Contents

Inhuman: Uncovering the Dark Truths of Psychopathy and Sociopathy

Subtle Shades – How to Distinguish Between Psychopaths and Sociopaths

The 17 Psyches of Psychopathy

Corporate Psychopaths: How They Scale the Ladder and Scale it FAST

Spotting the Danger- 20 Traits of a Functioning Psychopath

Seduction and Destruction - The Pathology of a Sexual Predator

Identifying Oddities in A Psychopath's Speech Patterns

How to Determine the Lies of a Psychopath

DOMINATE:

How Psychopaths Think, Act & Succeed

By C.K. Murray

Copyright © 2015 C.K. Murray

All Rights Reserved

Similar works by C.K. Murray:

Persuasion Explained: How to Use Your Inner Eye to Influence Others

Master Mind: Unleashing the Infinite Power of the Latent Brain

Sex Science: 21 SIZZLING Secrets That Will Transform Your Bedroom into a Sauna

Body Language Explained: How to Master the Power of the Unconscious

Master of the Game: A Modern Male's Guide to Sexual Conquest

You've met one before.

If not personally, at the very least in passing. Perhaps you've crossed paths every day. Maybe it's a neighbor or an acquaintance or a person at work. Or maybe it's somebody you've seen or heard, somebody who seems no different than you and I. Normally dressed, normally behaved, normally raised with a more or less normal background; a stranger but no danger...

Or so its seems.

Truth be told, they're everywhere. And many of them are looking down. The reason they're looking down is because they're above us, far above us, pulling the strings and making the calls. Positions of power, spheres of control. Puppet masters without remorse.

If they aren't 'everyday people,' they're something more. CEOs and chairmen and tycoons and politicians and leaders with thousands or millions of people at their disposal. With one rash decision, they can ruin the livelihoods of countless others. In one moment of thought, they can change everything for everyone.

Self-gain is the name of their game; and you better believe they're hellbent on winning.

But most people don't know it. Most people go through their lives, clueless, unaware, never once thinking that the gentle smile and pleasant face of a particular person is hiding something. Something so dark and disturbing, that to unleash its ugliness would destroy all illusions of normalcy.

Sociopaths are not like you and I. They don't *feel* the way you and I do, about life, about people, about places and things that orbit in and out of our busy worlds. Sociopaths are capable of feats that most of us cannot *begin* to comprehend. And the reason for this is simple.

Most of us have no idea. What it's like. To truly. Dominate...

Inhuman: Uncovering the Dark Truths of Psychopathy and Sociopathy

Nothing is what it seems.

This is especially true when it comes to psychopaths. Although many people would like to believe that they have an understanding of psychopaths, the truth is that most of us have no idea. This is a problem that stems not only from personal ignorance, but from a general misunderstanding of the term 'psychopath.'

Nowadays, psychopath and sociopath have become separate entities. While it's easy to confuse the two, not knowing the subtle differences between them, there are certainly many similarities. Considered legitimate mental disorders by the Diagnostic and Statistical Manual of Mental Disorders, 5th Edition (DSM V), psychopathy and sociopathy are now categorized under "Antisocial Personality Disorder." Both disorders are believed to start at around the age of 15, with symptoms often manifesting as an abnormal cruelty toward life. This typically begins with cruelty toward animals before working its way to a more sinister cruelty toward humans.

In both disorders, a lack of conscience, remorse or guilt for hurtful actions eventually manifests with alarming regularity. Although sociopaths and psychopaths understand social norms on an intellectual level, they tend to have no emotional connection. Due to this, many sociopaths and psychopaths are incapable of forming genuine relations with others.

According to the DSM-5, there are four diagnostic criteria for

Antisocial Personality Disorder, with criterion A requiring at least one of the sub-criteria:

A. Disregard for and violation of others rights since age 15, as indicated by one of the seven sub features:

1. Failure to obey laws and norms by engaging in behavior which results in criminal arrest, or would warrant criminal arrest

2. Lying, deception, and manipulation, for profit tor self-amusement,

3. Impulsive behavior

4. Irritability and aggression, manifested as frequently assaults others, or engages in fighting

5 Blatantly disregards safety of self and others,

6 A pattern of irresponsibility and

7. Lack of remorse for actions (American Psychiatric Association, 2013)

The other diagnostic Criterion are:

B. The person is at least age 18,

C. Conduct disorder was present by history before age 15

D. and the antisocial behavior does not occur in the context of schizophrenia or bipolar disorder (American Psychiatric Association, 2013)

Subtle Shades – How to Distinguish Between Psychopaths and Sociopaths

Can *you* spot the difference between a psychopath and sociopath? Do you have any idea?

In order to delineate the disorders, psychologists, psychiatrists and mental health experts have drawn a line in the sand. Although still categorized under the general antisocial personality disorder framework, the differences between psychopath and sociopath are very real. The critical distinctions are as follows:

	Psychopathy	**Sociopathy**
Diagnosis	Antisocial personality disorder; with emphasis on the lack of empathy	Antisocial personality disorder
Source	It is now believed that genetic anomalies lead to structural changes in the brain; psychopathy is caused by inherent problems in the brain	Sociopaths are believed to be socially constructed, through poor environments, lack of a support network, and exposure to violence
Proclivity for violence	High	Normal
Impulsiveness	Low	High
Criminality	Incredibly skilled at calculated, callous maneuvers that are often undiscovered by law enforcement; highly premeditated	Prone to impulsive criminal acts that are easier to uncover due to evidence; less careful at hiding evidence; notable risk takers; opportunistic

Social interactions	Incapable of forming genuine relationships; superficial relations are created for self-gain; cause hurt to others without emotional response	Very skilled at superficial relationships; typically experience some form of guilt when affecting those close

As you have noticed, the main differences between psychopaths and sociopaths are the origin of the mental disorder. Sociopaths are often reared in very troubling environments that are not conducive to normal development. Children may be abused, may witness violence, or may experience general negligence. Over time, these environments harden sociopaths to the feelings of others, creating violent tendencies.

Psychopaths, by comparison, may be even more disturbing. Their brains are believed to be wired differently from birth, essentially. Psychopaths are not impulsive, instead acting in very cold and calculated measures. Ulterior motives are often disguised incredibly well, and in most cases, psychopaths will *appear* to have others' best interests at heart.

Violence is another thing that psychopaths have mastered. Because they are adept at hiding evidence and distancing themselves, many psychopaths may not commit violence directly. Instead, they might deliver directives that end in violence. This way, they are able to wash their hands clean of culpability, preserving their image so that they can continue their antisocial behaviors.

The violence inhibition mechanism (VIM) is the system responsible for violent attitudes and behaviors in psychopaths. In basic functioning, the VIM is receptive to 'distress cues.' These distress cues occur when a person or thing is clearly in some kind of pain. Submissive gestures such as showing the neck, wrists, or other pleas for mercy are then interpreted by the VIM. In normal people, these cues will cause a threat response that ceases violent activities. This is why most people have an aversion to other people's pain, and to the thought of pain-inducing acts. Most people will show mercy, whether by not participating in violence, or by restricting the violence at a certain point.

In the psychopath's mind, however, the VIM does not react this way. Instead, there is no threat response, and the psychopath experiences no aversion to suffering. Brain scans support this. In many scans of psychopathic brains, there is limited, if any, activity in the areas associated with empathy, compassion, mercy, and the like. Put simply, psychopaths do not feel what you and I do. It's not merely that they don't care about others; it's that they don't have the *capacity* to care.

Contrary to common belief, psychopaths are not psychotic. They do not suffer from hallucinations or delusions. They are very firmly rooted in reality, so much so, that they understand full-on the repercussions of their actions, even if they don't *feel* them. Another thing to note is the violent proclivities of psychopaths. Most of them are not serial killers or murderers. For those that engage in violent behavior, it usually takes the form of coercion, threats, intimidation and domination. Most violence, while an effective tool in the psychopath's arsenal, is not fatal.

Still, sometimes violence is the least of our worries. When it comes to psychopathy, there are numerous faces. The person you consider your best friend can become your worst enemy. Those you think you know, have the most to hide...

The 17 Psyches of Psychopathy

No two psychopaths are the same. In fact, there are numerous types and expression of psychopathy, all of them sharing a distinct rejection of human sensitivity. Deficits in emotion such as guilt, remorse, empathy, compassion, and morality all remain intact—but other aspects are vastly different. Let's consider the various psyches of psychopathy:

The Deceiver

Known as "pathological liars," these psychopaths often lie for no apparent reason. They are skilled at lying and have been doing so from their earliest years. However, because they lie frequently, they may occasionally get caught in their own web. If they forget what they told to one person vs. another person, their falsehoods may be discovered. Even so, they do not care at all about this discovery.

To this psychopath, the concept of truth means nothing. They have no conception of what it means to be honest or true. There is what one person believes and what another person believes, but to the psychopath, neither of those stances are objectively 'true' or 'false.' They are merely words, constructed for reasons.

These psychopaths will say what they want to get what they want. Oftentimes they begin to believe their own deceptive statements, losing track of what is actually true. They will say what others want to hear, show the side that others want to see, and play the part—whatever part—to reach the desired outcome. This could mean lying for money, for help, for a job, to get out of legal trouble, to appease somebody else, etc. To this psychopath, there is no such thing as telling the truth. There is only telling the tale.

The Victim

This psychopath is adept at playing the losing hand. In other words, this psychopath will pretend to be down-and-out in life. In order to elicit the sympathy and empathy of others, the Victim will act broken, lost, and highly incapable. He or she may tell others how much they mean, offering them high praises for their relative success in life. Whenever possible, the Victim will resort to self-demeaning statements in order to sustain the help and compassion of others.

The Victim is highly effective for several reasons. Many people may decide to help, believing that they are doing a good thing in assisting a needy person. Of course, many times the Victim actually requires nothing. Most of these psychopaths have created or exaggerated their poor circumstances. They meticulously choose their outfits, mannerisms, and words so that they communicate a subordinate social, economic, emotional and mental position. By doing this, they can often glob off of others without ever having to do anything for themselves.

For the psychopath, the decision is made dispassionately. Why work hard in life when financial stability can be achieved by manipulating someone else?

The Sex Fiend

These psychopaths are especially dangerous to women, but have been known to also appear in certain female subsets. Characterized by hypersexual urges and perversions, the Sex

Fiend will engage frequently in activities such as fetishes, incest, homosexuality, exhibitionism, voyeurism, and pornography.

When engaging targets, this sexual psychopath will become an obvious predator. Oftentimes, they pride themselves on the ability to dominate, manipulate, and violate the weaker victim. Many of them are serial rapists and stalkers, forcing their victims to appease their twisted desires in unfathomable acts of self-subjugation.

Many of these psychopaths locate targets indiscriminately. They may be pedophiles or they may be serial rapists, but oftentimes, they are willing to sexually exploit anyone of any age—children, teenagers, adults, elders; boys and girls, women and men; heterosexuals and homosexuals; able-bodied and disabled. It doesn't matter. They are emotionally unmoved by what they do and will carry out their terrible deeds with clinical precision.

The Social Victor

This psychopath has one clear goal: to ascend the social ladder. Whether at work or among important social circles, this psychopath places social esteem above everything else. In order to ascend the ladder, this psychopath employs a variety of intelligent tactics. Firstly, he or she will be exceedingly well-spoken and gregarious, often winning the adulation of numerous others.

At work, this person can cunningly display all the winning attributes. Even if the truth is far different, the Social Victor will appear to be hard working, reliable, steadfast, and well-intended. This facade of sociability and friendliness is so carefully crafted, that the vast majority of people will never see through it. Executives and persons of power will receive the Social Victor's best acting, which is how this psychopath scales the ladders so quickly.

The Torturer

This psychopath will dominate all others through violent means. Lack of mercy and humanness characterize this nefarious type, meaning that the weakest victims are often selected first. These psychopaths target those who will submit in order to inflict continuous violence and psychological torture. The main goal in carrying out such violent acts is to disseminate terror and suffering. The more vulnerable the target, the better. The Torturer will continue to derive meaning from the torturous acts inflicted; that is, until a new target has been located.

With the Torturer, the name of the game is power. And nothing says power more than the pained pleas of a helpless human.

The 'One'

This psychopath type will act perfectly in order to make us feel special beyond special. Often male, this psychopath will present as the ideal mate, a caring, loving, ever-faithful partner that will share our interests, our loves, and our deepest desires for a 'soul-mate.' This psychopath crafts an aura of relaxation and trust, causing us to drop our guard and succumb. They may serve us hand and foot. They may come to us in our greatest moments of weakness, assuaging our fears, insecurities, and other emotional issues.

Their charm is endlessly attractive.

But then it ends. Once the romantic scenarios and loving discussions fade away, the truth reveals itself. This psychopath merely said and did what was necessary to get you. In many cases, he or she pretended to like you or share your interests, anything to win you over. Once you are won and secured, the psychopath will reveal its true nature. The psychopath will become selfish and abusive, quickly and incredibly transforming before your eyes. The person you thought you loved, the one you married, will become somebody you never once envisioned: a manipulative, uncaring, shell of a human. And now, with your lives so intertwined, you'll realize that you have sacrificed your own identity for this person. For the person you thought you knew.

And if you seek help, if you dare contact somebody out of fear or uncertainty, the psychopath will know. And once the psychopath becomes aware of your efforts to 'get out' of the relationship, the physical, mental and emotional suffering will begin in earnest.

The Thrill

Psychopaths are typically low in impulsiveness, but this type defies the mold. Bent on chasing thrill after dangerous thrill, this psychopath is unaffected by frightening, risky, uncertain events. Forever pursuing stimulation, the Thrill cares not for the consequences of his or her capricious acts. The extent to which this psychopath will ignore the effects on others is pathological. There is no responsibility and accountability, meaning that the Thrill will continue to destroy him or herself—as well as those around—for the sheer sake of excitement. When drugs and alcohol are thrown into the mix, this psychopath will take to completely new extremes. The only goal is simple: continue to live without boundaries, notwithstanding destructive repercussions.

The Intellectual

These psychopaths will pursue positions of academic relevance. Oftentimes, they are doctors, lawyers, psychologists, university professors, and specialists in other fields. Many of these psychopaths get into their respective positions through deception and fraud. They may fake their qualifications and credentials in order to gain the office of their choosing. They are very adept at adopting the diction and formal trappings of academic work, oftentimes communicating their perceived superiority through fancy discourse.

They are not keen on being anybody's friend. They demean others through ornate language, prey on students and subordinates—often sexually—and have no qualms about disappearing when their deception is exposed. For those psychopaths who *do* get to their positions honestly, the focus is on using those positions for manipulation. In professions such as doctors and professors, psychopaths may needlessly prescribe drugs, endlessly impart extremist ideas, and generally exploit the system for their gain.

The Artist

Many artists like to push the boundaries and think outside the box. For this reason, the psychopath can easily assimilate to artistic circles. By adopting the counterculture mindset among many writers, artists and revolutionaries, this psychopath can intermingle almost seemingly without suspicion. In many cases, the dark, disturbing mind of this psychopath is disguised behind notions of 'creative genius.'

The Artist is typically hellbent on removing moral imperative. By rejecting qualities such as respect, kindness and fairness, this psychopath will embark on a journey of liberation. Through clever pseudo-intellectual claims, the Artist can convince many a fellow bohemian of the need for counter-qualities: perversion, inequality, disrespect and selfishness. Only by letting loose the darkness, the Artist claims, will true enlightenment be achieved.

The Envious

We've all been envious or jealous of somebody else—this is human nature. But with this psychopath, such envy and jealousy become pathological. The psychopath craves restitution for perceived wrongs. Whether the psychopath believes others have forsaken him, or that the design of life itself has played foul, it doesn't matter. What matters to this psychopath is reclaiming what he or she believes is 'owed.'

By engaging in theft, destruction, and general deceit, this psychopath will try to rectify the life-inflicted wrongs of destiny. The spectrum can range from stealing small possessions or garnering minor reparations, to completely and ravenously destroying the successes of others. It can be a material destruction or an unraveling of immaterial markers like partners and career—what matters is that the psychopath removes it. By removing the power of others, the psychopath revels in the downfall.

However, these psychopaths are rarely satisfied. They are perpetually empty, striving without ultimate success to fill themselves with the 'gifts' of others. In the end, the psychopath continues to steal, destroy and usurp those deemed undeserving. And with each step toward that final attainment, the pathological greed, jealousy and envy only intensify.

The Killer

This is the stereotypical murderer/serial killer. Think Jeffrey Dahmer or Ted Bundy. These psychopaths are generally very normal. They pay their bills, say hi to their neighbors, smile, laugh and relate like anybody else. To the untrained eye, these cunning chameleons will seem anything but dangerous.

But the truth runs deep. In reality, they care naught for others. They have been different since childhood, often incapable of conscience. Their relentless, calculated desire for death is often an attempt to make up for years of torment. As young children, some of these serial killers lived in less than hospitable environments. Some of them may have been orphans, others had abusive parents, and some still came from completely normal upbringings.

In all of these killers, a profound deprivation and desire for retribution abound. They will revel in the continued and meticulous suffering of their victims, fueling their underlying feelings of frustration, resentment and anger Of course, the suffering is just part of the fun. These psychopaths may collect remnants of their victims as trinkets; reminders of the power they exerted.

Even so, these malevolent psychopaths do have limits. They understand what can and can't be done, but will often push to the extreme as much as they can. While they understand moral concepts rationally and can explain why society feels certain ways, these psychopaths cannot *feel* those mores. This is one of the main reasons for their nature.

The Silent

As the title suggests, this psychopath is quiet. Typically withdrawn and detached, this psychopath is highly introverted. Usually ragged or uncleanly in appearance, the Silent will have no interest in being nice or friendly, and thus will create relationships built solely on negative feelings. This usually means hurting, harming, or rejecting others prematurely in order to avoid future failures. If they can hurt you before you disappoint them, they have won. Violent acts may occur simultaneously to damage those the psychopath finds threatening.

The Demagogue

You have seen these before. They appear in politics, religion, and other opportunistic spheres. If you've ever witnessed a motivational speaker, a religious zealot, or some form of grandstander, you've probably witnessed the Demagogue. The main ploy of the Demagogue is to appeal to your emotions over your rationale. This psychopath will say what you want to hear, oftentimes communicating exaggerated personal experiences of change and new-found happiness or success. In most cases, the Demagogue seeks nothing more than your attention, your subservience, and your charitable donations. Money and manipulation mean everything to this psychopath; more often than not, these goals are reached through emotional appeal. An appeal to the naive, the weak and the vulnerable.

The Paranoid

When paranoid delusions mix with psychopathy, watch out!

This mentally mangled psychopath will eventually 'suspect' everybody. Disconnected events and details will be aligned in the psychopath's mind, creating causal links that any sober mind would find completely nonsensical. The Paranoid is perpetually distrusting, blaming others for uncontrolled events, projecting feelings onto others, and creating a reality in which others are cunningly deceptive.

In the mind of this psychopath, all others are part of a complicated system of subterfuge and malevolence. This *imagined* insidious intent leads the psychopath to increasingly withdraw from reality. Sooner than later, the Paranoid will believe that others are hellbent on intimidating, offending and controlling the psychopath's mind. As a result, the psychopath will begin to plan ahead. He or she will manage these 'evil' acts by countering with evil acts. In the end, the psychopath may become a complete recluse, terrorizing by night and vanishing by day.

The Textbook

No, this psychopath is not an academic. The "textbook" in the title refers to this type's stereotypical traits. Defined clearly by the American Diagnostic and Statistical Manual (DSM), this type is best encapsulated under the "antisocial personality disorder" tag. They comprise the majority of prison-mates, and are frequently in trouble with the law for violent acts, petty crimes, and other destructive, antisocial behaviors.

The DSM defines this types as being deceitful, impulsive, reckless, aggressive, irresponsible and lacking in remorse. There is often a conspicuous lack of disregard for lawful behavior, a pattern of lying, evasion and aliases, repeated incidences of physical altercations, inconsistent work behavior, and an indifference toward others' feelings.

The Snake Oil Salesman

These psychopaths will try to 'sell' you anything. Whether it be tales of their past, victim-hood stories, visions of success and prosperity, their pain and suffering, or an actual, tangible product or service—the Snake Oil Salesman is trying to sell. The reason these psychopaths want to sell you something is simple: it will get them ahead.

Although they may artfully persuade others that the product or service is of mutual gain, this is often far from the truth. The Snake Oil Salesman relies on several assumptions to make their sales. Firstly, they need you to like them, which means they will be witty, kind, and pretend to empathize. These psychopaths are highly <u>emotionally intelligent</u>, meaning that they can manipulate quite readily. For that reason, they will always expect something in return. If they are giving you a great 'deal,' it's because they expect you to buy. They don't want to help you; they want to help themselves!

Snake Oil Salesmen will make their pitch by comparing you to others. They may tell you that many others have already made a purchase, that the product or service is of superior quality for this reason. The Snake Oil Salesman will claim to be all-knowing about the product or service, convincing you that their knowledge on the topic makes them an expert. "You can trust me, I know, I'm looking out for you."

The truly psychopathic nature of the Snake Oil Salesman will occasionally surface under extreme duress. If continuously denied, the salesmen may abandon a pitch and instead rely on intimidation and coercion. The charismatic, understanding facade will shatter, revealing a ruthless antagonist. In the end, smart pitches and persuasive arguments will give way to veiled or even outright threats and ultimatums.

"If you don't make this purchase, right here, right now, I swear to God I'll make you regret it..."

The Moral Arbiter

This psychopath will act holier-than-thou and view most others as immoral and undeserving. By proclaiming the need for justice and fairness, this psychopath *appears* to be concerned with general well-being. Unfortunately, this alleged position of moral superiority is based upon one need: the need to deceive, abuse, corrupt and control. Most of these psychopaths will position themselves as religious leaders, educators, and managers of places such as hospitals and recreational centers. They will stick to their fixed moral system, espousing their beliefs to the naive and harmless.

As the Moral Arbiter, this psychopath is obsessed with image. This is why they will often have their close friends and families lie on their behalf, while presenting an array of accolades and achievements (oftentimes faked) in order to prove their moral high ground. Those who stand to block them from ascension are quickly cut down.

The important thing to remember is that every psychopath has a different face. Every psyche is different. What makes one psychopath tick may do nothing for another. Just like you and I, not all psychopaths are created equal. Although they all engage in antisocial behaviors, their reasons for doing so can differ vastly. One may be violent, another may not be. And in many cases, the most dangerous psychopaths—the ones that destroy the most people—do not have to rely on violence at all...

Corporate Psychopaths: How They Scale the Ladder and Scale it FAST

The facts are alarming. According to most experts, roughly 15% of prisoners are psychopaths. And roughly 1% of the general public are psychopaths.

But the worst psychopaths, the most powerful—the puppet masters of psychopathy—are the ones of business. Studies show that about 3% of those in the upper rungs of business are psychopathic. Unlike the popular idea of crazy, teeth-chattering killers, these dangerous psychopaths are hard to spot. They possess incredible charisma, charming coworkers and friends and drawing admirers from far and wide.

In the corporate world, it is easy to mistake their defining traits for nothing more than a business drive. Smart, decisive, cool and collected, these psychopaths appear to be nothing more than motivated careerists. However, it is these highly-touted business traits that also serve to exacerbate psychopathy. Because these individuals are often highly intelligent and socially connected, they have the perfect recipe for ascension. They can manipulate, becoming remorseless in their unethical cutthroat tactics. When approached about ethical or moral dilemmas, the corporate psychopath will minimize the gravity of such measures. Instead, they will calmly emphasize the importance of their 'business acumen,' explaining away any transgressions as mere byproducts of the corporate process.

In ascending the business ladder, the corporate psychopath will cleanly plant an array of falsehoods, white lies, and disingenuous statements. The psychopath may even embroil others in fake controversy, creating an atmosphere in which he or she can become the unassuming coworker—above any and all suspicion.

The corporate psychopath is no stranger to faking records, resumes, accounts, transactions, and other pertinent financial information. In all cases, the slant of such doctored documents will favor the psychopath. Hyper-competitive by nature, the corporate psychopath is perpetually motivated to self-aggrandize. All efforts are directed toward one goal: achievement. If others stand in the way of that achievement, they will be dealt with in a swift but subtle manner.

The reason the corporate psychopath can handle people so well is due to an inhuman ability for reading people. They are skilled masters of body language, ensuring that they can tell what you're thinking even when you tell them otherwise. They spend many minutes and hours observing those around them, identifying weaknesses, motives, needs, desires, and soft spots. Given their heightened communication skills, corporate psychopaths move like chameleons from one conversation to another. They do not fear an inability to 'fit in,' because they have never known what that is like. Fluid in persona and psyche, these talented beguilers will employ superficial conversations in order to win their way into your circle of trust. Once inside, they will destroy you from the inside out.

Still, before they get inside, you can take steps to ensure that your boundaries are strong. Notice the following traits in a corporate psychopath and thwart him or her before it's too late:

Drive

Psychopaths are undeterred by feelings of guilt or remorse. Without a capacity for empathy, they can ignore emotional concerns in favor of cold rationality. To the psychopath, the job is a job. They don't care who they have to hurt or destroy to get their promotion, their paycheck, their vacation, retirement, etc. All they care about is making that next call, sealing that next deal, cornering that next client into a position of utter vulnerability. They can become so focused on business, that nothing else matters. Even health and well-being may become secondary concerns in the face of looming financial gain.

Intrepidity

Psychopaths are not affected by fear like you and I. They don't fear taking a chance. They can make cold calls without effort because they do not fear being turned down or saying the wrong thing. They do not fear taking on a big new project or cutting corners to get what they want. No matter what deceptive steps they take, corporate psychopaths are not afraid of repercussion.

Lack of empathy

Again, psychopaths lack empathy. But that doesn't mean they don't fake it. The good corporate psychopaths almost always have the biggest smiles and deepest laughs. They are geniuses at adopting the right body language and business jargon. They are not afraid to screw you over if they know they can get away with it. And when they *are* found out, they'll quickly cut all ties. The business relationship you thought you shared with them, will suddenly disappear.

Self-confidence

Psychopaths have no fear of going alone. They assume themselves superior anyway, so this narcissism is naturally conducive to isolation. Psychopaths will approach upper management without nerves and anxiety. They'll regale big clients with worldly tales, they'll deliver bold-faced lies in speeches and boardroom discussions, they'll play up values important to their bosses, such as honesty, respect, integrity, and family. They may even pretend to have certain skill-sets, even when in reality they have no experience whatsoever in that particular area.

Psychopaths will continue to function in a world where they are the primary benefactors. That is their world—their perception. Everything revolves for them. The sun rises so that they too may rise, and conquer, the weaklings before them. The corporate psychopath will not tolerate those who try to stop them. If you are an honest competitor, they will undermine you. If you are their boss, they will wow you. If you are a coworker in passing, they may never acknowledge you.

Or they may *always* acknowledge you, waiting for the perfect day to manipulate you with a big, gleaming smile...

Spotting the Danger- 20 Traits of a Functioning Psychopath

The problem with psychopaths is their intelligence and their incapacity to care. For this reason, even the most obvious behaviors may go unnoticed if the psychopath is cunning enough. And many CEOs, board members, and upper management heads *are* cunning enough. That's how they got to where they are. As such, it takes more than simply a careful observation of behaviors. In order to fully identify psychopaths, a more advanced metric is required.

This is why Robert Hare devised the Hare Psychopathy Checklist, a 20 item inventory that assesses the probability of psychopathic tendency. Used by law enforcement and clinicians worldwide, this assessment instrument utilizes a three point scale. Each item can be assigned a score of either 0, 1, or 2. Zero means that the item does not apply, 1 means that there is a partial relevance, and 2 means that there is a reasonably good match. With a maximum score of 40, the cut-off for psychopathy is 30 in the United States and 25 in the United Kingdom. Interestingly, these cultural differences reflect differences in the traits both cultures condone and promote. Given the American drive for personal success, it is no surprise that the cut-off score is higher.

The 20 items are as follows:

1. GLIB and SUPERFICIAL CHARM - smooth talking and verbally adept. Never at a loss for something to say, and not afraid to say anything.

2. GRANDIOSE SELF-WORTH - There is an opinion for even the most trivial things, and a constant braggadocios nature about things done, achieved, and expected to do. The ego is a central

element, meaning that self-focus is the norm. Confidence and arrogance abound.

3. SEEK STIMULATION or PRONE TO BOREDOM - Are never satisfied and move on indiscriminately to the next exciting venture. Never engage in things deemed boring and are prone to doing and saying things that are risky by nature.

4. PATHOLOGICAL LYING - Beyond normal lying. This includes lying in situations where being caught is likely. The automatic nature of lying is such that it may not even be realized.

5. CONNING AND MANIPULATIVENESS - Natural-born con artists. Excel at deceiving, cheating, tricking and defrauding for personal gain. The effect on others does not register.

6. LACK OF REMORSE OR GUILT - Remain dispassionate, cold-hearted, and unaffected. A disdain for victims may lead to conclusions that they had it coming or somehow deserved it.

7. SHALLOW AFFECT - Superficial emotional responses; simply going through the motions. Very shallow feelings and a distance from others. May seem friendly but in reality have no connection. Cold and detached.

8. CALLOUSNESS and LACK OF EMPATHY - A general inability to experience interpersonal feelings. Indifference may become downright alienation.

9. PARASITIC LIFESTYLE - Will quickly glob onto others or exploit others for self-gain. Have no qualms about manipulating the vulnerable and take no responsibility for said manipulation.

10. POOR BEHAVIORAL CONTROLS - Occasional outbursts that are noticeably out of character. These sudden expressions of

anger, hostility, irritation and the like may lead to rash and damaging decisions.

11. PROMISCUOUS SEXUAL BEHAVIOR - Rarely sustain a meaningful relationship. Multiple sexual encounters and affairs. Many times, relationships are heterosexual, homosexual or anything else. Women are likely to be coerced into deprived sexual acts, and such coercions are often remembered by the psychopath as boast-worthy conquests. May sustain several relationships at once.

12. EARLY BEHAVIOR PROBLEMS - Typically starts at 15, but can be reported much earlier. Problem behaviors include lying, theft, cheating in school, property damage, absenteeism, drug use, physical altercations and sexual activity. Cruelty to animals and/or siblings is a constant.

13. LACK OF REALISTIC, LONG-TERM GOALS - May discuss grandiose schemes or trajectories, but rarely follow through. There is a conspicuous inability to reach goals, and a clear lack of direction.

14. IMPULSIVITY - Behaviors are sometimes unplanned. Regardless of consequences, instant gratification becomes a central obsession.

15. IRRESPONSIBILITY - Commitment and duties mean nothing. May fail to do many things we are all expected to do, such as care for family and kids, pay bills, go to work, attend events, and so on.

16. FAILURE TO ACCEPT RESPONSIBILITY FOR OWN ACTIONS - Responsibility is denied at all costs. Responsibility is instead heaped on others' shoulders, even when others have no bearing in the situation. Highly unaccountable.

17. MANY SHORT-TERM MARITAL RELATIONSHIPS - Lack of reliability leads to difficulty sustaining marriage. Adulterous behaviors also affect this.

18. JUVENILE DELINQUENCY - Behavioral troubles from ages 13-18. Whether petty crimes or more serious, behaviors exhibit a blatant disregard for social norms.

19. REVOCATION OF CONDITION RELEASE - Inability to follow directives leads to legal problems with conditions such as probation, parole, mandatory meetings, etc. In most cases, carelessness it to blame.

20. CRIMINAL VERSATILITY - An ability to navigate various criminal fronts while staying effective at obscuring evidence. Great pride is derived from diverse criminal activity; superiority to criminal 'specialists' is exhibited.

The most important thing to remember is that psychopaths are not going to diagnose themselves. In fact, that is the irony of the psychopath. They are so deluded, so self-involved, that they may not even see the wrong in their ways. In their minds, what they are doing is what they should be doing; what they *have* to do, even.

And this reality becomes all the more scary when you consider a certain breed of psychopath. That is, the sexual predator...

Seduction and Destruction - The Pathology of a Sexual Predator

With most people, sex means something.

Maybe it's an act that we consider fun or thrilling. Maybe it's a way to show our feelings for another person. Maybe it's merely an animalistic desire that we act on. But by and large, sex—and the science of sex—are important aspects of our lives.

For most people, sex is emotional and mutual. For psychopaths, sex is neither. With psychopaths, sex is no more than a way to further exercise power and dominion. Unlike romantic relationships and strong emotional bonds, psychopathic sex is an act achieved through calculated moves and maneuvers. Instead of developing organic chemistry with another person, the psychopath is playing a game.

And more often than not, they'll win with flying colors.

This happens because psychopaths crave power beyond all else. When a male psychopath seduces a woman, he is preying on a very real set of cues. He will notice her body language, her verbal variance, her gestures, facial expressions, and micro-movements. He will flatter her, seeming urbane and confident, knowing when to lie his hand upon her shoulder, when to touch the small of her back, how to gently lean in, how to kiss her slowly at first and gradually work his way, stoking the flames of lust with intense delay.

Many psychopaths are skilled at intercourse. They have mastered the art of performance, knowing when to apologize, how to confess their 'love,' and where to position themselves when making love to a woman. They are often fierce and powerful in the bed, commanding the female body with interchanging grace, sensitivity, and authority.

However, there are often warning signs. Whether a male psychopath or a female psychopath, the goal is simple: to eradicate barriers and exploit vulnerabilities. And what's a more vulnerable time than the moment of post-coitus, when both partners are naked in bed?

Psychopaths know who to target. They'll seduce wealthy individuals, weak and lost women and men, those rebounding from a relationship and feeling valueless, and an array of other insecure and sexually receptive persons of interest.

Psychopaths are skilled at being in the right place at the right time. This is why they will frequent bars, restaurants, clubs and other social settings where the lubricating effect of alcohol can take effect. Once tipsy or inebriated, many people begin to give away subtle indicators of their intentions. At this point, an interested psychopath will approach, head high, eyes focused. They will come across as excessively flattering and relatable. From the very start, they will stare you right in the eye and pretend to understand you on a deep, fundamental level. They will lie to mimic your own experiences, attitudes and beliefs. They will also assess your level of receptiveness and vulnerability by asking deep and personal questions from the very start.

In most cases, we get a feeling that the psychopath is, in fact, not a normal person. The fact that they come on so strong and seem so determined to get us home is usually a giveaway. However, most of us may ignore this automatic alert because we are lonely, or sad, or depressed, or curious, or simply aroused. Many times we simply want to believe that we've experienced "love at first sight," that we've finally found 'the one.' More often than not, however, we succumb because we're creatures of emotion.

Psychopaths are not.

And we learn this eventually. Psychopaths will use men or women as sexual objects and then discard them. They will demean the man or woman for a period, stringing them along until the psychopath has moved on. Ironically, this uncaring attitude toward the target may cause that man or woman to feel strangely attracted. It isn't until the man or woman is abruptly abandoned, that the missed warning signs become clear.

Fortunately, there *are* ways to tell if a psychopath is targeting you, in real-time. If you aren't sure if you've encountered or will encounter a psychopath, be sure to know the drill. If a psychopath is bent on manipulation, there are certain patterns that occur. And these patterns, even a psychopath cannot fully hide...

Identifying Oddities in A Psychopath's Speech Patterns

One landmark study has revealed that psychopaths differ from us normal folk in one very telling way. This difference, it turns out, is directly tied to their speech and mannerisms. Although psychopaths are known for their evident lack of affect, they can and do readily engage in patterns that distinguish them.

Unlike the rest of us, psychopaths show no difference in their voice volume, intonation, inflection or tonality when using neutral and emotional words. Most of us emphasize emotional words, or words referring to emotionally-charged events. With psychopaths, these words are expressed in flat, emotionless fashion. However, psychopaths are very skilled at faking that emotion when they have to. They can cry their way to lesser punishments in court, and plead with police officers for exceptions to be made when caught for petty disturbances and misdemeanors.

In general, speech pattern software has analyzed psychopathic speech with surprising results. Analyses show that psychopaths tend to talk of fulfilling basic needs, such as eating, drinking and spending money. In fact, many psychopaths are known to discuss mundane details just as they discuss murder details during interrogations. This is because psychopaths are incapable of expressing the emotional difference between violent atrocities and everyday tasks like cleaning the dishes. However, psychopaths are less likely to talk about other things, such as family and friends. This makes sense, since psychopaths are not capable of forming lasting relationships anyway.

Criminal investigators have also found that psychopaths use more past-tense words when describing events, especially during violent narratives. This indicates a detachment from the event, as if it occurred a long time ago and has no bearing on the present. When telling stories, a lot of people may talk as if the event is occurring in the present, saying things such as "So I'm about to do *x*" or "I'm at my place, getting ready" or "At this point, I'm thinking." Most people talk this way because they feel a connection in the present to what happened, and are—in a way—reliving that experience by telling it. To a psychopath, this is not the case. What happened, happened, and the psychopath will coldly move on.

Although the psychopath often speaks in hollow tones, when trying to manipulate, they will adopt all the necessary tonal shifts. However, they will still display certain tendencies. Psychopaths often employ subordinating conjunctions, such as "because" and "so that," in order to indicate a logical cause and effect,. This means that the psychopath views his or her actions as necessary for completing whatever cold, calculated, nefarious mission is on the schedule. In addition to these conjunctions, psychopaths also use a variety of "uhs" and "ums" in their speech. Although this would seem to contradict the nature of psychopathy—advanced verbal skills—experts think that the "um" and "uhs" are voluntary. An attempt, if you will, to seem a little more normal.

How to Determine the Lies of a Psychopath

And therein lies the problem. When do we ever know, really, if the psychopath is deceiving us? How do we know if a psychopathic psyche is resting behind those dazzling, trustful eyes; behind that gentle, easy smile; behind the words, the nods, the expressions on those perfect features...

How do we know?

Well, we know because we learn. And we learn because we note the physical changes that tell us the truth when a psychopath is telling a tale.

They are:

Reply Speed

This refers to the speed of a response. Was it fast or slow? Did it change speed at any time or was it constant? Research shows that abnormally fast responses are probably premeditated, not necessarily meaning a lie, but at the very least indicating the person was wary enough to plan ahead. The opposite behavior—a very slow response—could be an attempt to create a believable reply.

Fidgeting

Lying shows up in nervous bouts of energy for most of us. In order to release this energy, we shift, move, shuffle, shift, and generally manipulate our bodies—often unconsciously. The feet and legs often stretch, curl and may even kick out as if to indicate that the liar is trying to run away. People also like to touch their shoes, clench their fists, rub their clothing, and generally include some nearby object so as to diffuse their anxiety through it.

Body Alignment & Movement

Deceitful people will often lean back their bodies so as to distance themselves from you. This unconscious mechanism serves as a defensive response. Crossed arms also signify discomfort and defensive posturing. These physical signs typically indicate a willingness to place psychological distance between one's true intentions and one's alleged intentions.

Many liars may try to compensate for unconscious movements by keeping their bodies rigid and still. This inhumanly still posture is common to psychopaths, who are highly aware of how their gestures may come across. In most cases, psychopaths do not consciously choose to sit still. It's just that their brains do not respond to emotion the ways ours do, so a question that would cause you or I to fidget nervously, will have no effect on a psychopath. Still, keep an eye out for micro-expressions, which are momentary dead giveaways to an individual's true intent. Be wary. They happen extremely fast, but can be very telling. If a smiling person tells you that you are forgiven, but the eyes flicker with anger, you might want to reconsider...

Fake Smile

Not all smiles are created equal. Smiles that don't extend to the eyes and form crinkles at the corners are not genuine. A fake smile only changes the mouth.

Pupil Changes

Liars experience pupil dilation. This is believed to occur because lies require extra concentration, as well as increased tension. Liars also blink at different rates, with slow blink rates during the lie, followed by rapid blinking afterward.

Nervous Touching

Believe it or not, the typical person will touch their face between 2,000 and 4,000 times each day. In deceiving persons, this touching is specific and will usually focus around the nose or lips just prior to delivering a lie. Partially concealing the eyes is another telltale sign. The reason this touching happens is because it is actually a subconscious effort to hide the truth—the physical manifestation of a psychological act.

Obfuscation

One of the telltale signs of liars is an inability to deliver a concise response. If you've ever watched a person stutter or struggle to give an honest answer, then you know. In many cases, the liar will begin by rambling, fumbling, or selectively responding to only parts of the question. He or she may rephrase the question, may use synonyms, or may qualify statements with things such as "I think" or "as far as I can remember" or "to my knowledge." A liar's vocal tone will also typically increase when compared to an honest person's tone. Liars will also avoid contractions in order to highlight the "not." This makes them seem more honest and direct. It also emphasizes the disconnect from any culpability. Such replies may be: "I do *not* remember that happening" instead of "I *don't* remember that happening."

Well there you have it, some of the more telling signs of a deceiving psychopath. It's important to remember, however, that psychopaths are good at what they do. Because they can easily hide true feelings, it is up to you to be on your best attention. If you can spot something, even for a split second, you might want to act on it. Oftentimes our instincts tell us something about a person, but we ignore them, instead trying to rationalize why we feel the way we do.

Trust your 'gut.' If you think that somebody is deceiving you or somebody else—don't delay. Do not be trusting to people who seem to have no fear. If a person is exceedingly charming, right off the bat—without knowing anything about you—consider the possibility of deception or manipulation. Many psychopaths will try to 'warm us up' in order to get to our true feelings and exploit them.

In moments of need, our worst enemies appear as our best friends.

What this book has tried to instill in you is an understanding of the psychopathic process. As you have learned, there are numerous faces of psychopathy. One one end, there are people bent on killing without remorse, and on the other end, puppet-masters who will stop at nothing for a promotion at Target.

Not all psychopaths are going to resort to violence, just as not all psychopaths live in solitary confinement in the middle of the mountains somewhere. Psychopaths have almost as much variability as the general population, and this is because they can *fake it* better than anyone else. You might go your whole life and never know that you met a psychopath. You might spend years in and out of different communities, neighborhoods, cities and townships, never once realizing that your friendly next door neighbor was a depraved sexual predator.

The important thing to remember is this: Know the signs,

understand the pathology, and react accordingly. The good news is, the overwhelming majority of everyday people are not psychopaths. Most of us are the 99%ers. We do not prey on others, and we damn well know what it *feels* like to experience strong emotion.

Most of us are good people, just trying to get by and enjoy our lives and those we care about.

But some of us, lurking, scheming, and hiding in plain sight— *some* of us are a different breed. And it is this different breed, this alien in disguise, that can bring us to our knees. So become the smart one, the strong one, and do not succumb their domination. Your life might just depend on it...

A Special Note:

Thank you for reading "*DOMINATE: How Psychopaths Think, Act & Succeed.*" If you enjoyed reading this book and would like to be included on an email list for when similar content is available, feel free:

SUBSCRIBE

As always, thank you for reading.

And may you continue to live healthily and happily.

Sincerely,

C.K. Murray

Other works by C.K. Murray:

1. *Mindfulness Explained: The Mindful Solution to Stress, Depression, and Chronic Unhappiness*

2. *Emotional Intelligence Explained: How to Master Emotional Intelligence and Unlock Your True Ability*

3. *The Confidence Cure: Your Definitive Guide to Overcoming Low Self-Esteem, Learning Self-Love and Living Happily*

4. *Let Love Flourish: The Secret to Finding Your Kindred Heart*

5. *Hair Loss Explained: Natural Solutions for Hair Loss and Premature Balding*

6. *The Omega Factor: 20 SUPERCHARGED Omega-3 Recipes for the Body and Mind*

7. *A Reason to Smile: Finding Happiness in Life's Little Moments*

8. *Health Hacks: 46 Hacks to Improve Your Mood, Boost Your Performance, and Guarantee a Longer, Healthier, More Vibrant Life*

9. *Depression, Drugs, & the Bottomless Pit: How I found my light amid the dark*

10. *The Stress Fallacy: Why Everything You Know Is WRONG*

11. *Master Mind: Unleashing the Infinite Power of the Latent Brain*

12. *Sex Science: 21 SIZZLING Secrets That Will Transform Your Bedroom into a Sauna*

13. *Sex Secrets: How to Conquer the Power of Sexual Attraction*

14. *Master of the Game: A Modern Male's Guide to Sexual Conquest*

15. *Persuasion Explained: How to Use Your Inner Eye to Influence Others*

16. *Deep Sleep: 32 Proven Tips for Deeper, Longer, More Rejuvenating Sleep*

17. *Win Back Your Ex! The Secrets to Rekindling Your Relationship*

18. *The Blood Pressure Diet: 30 Recipes Proven for Lowering Blood Pressure, Losing Weight, and Controlling Hypertension*

19. *Coconut Oil Cooking: 30 Delicious and Easy Coconut Oil Recipes Proven to Increase Weight Loss and Improve Overall Health*

20. *High Blood Pressure Explained: Natural, Effective, Drug-Free Treatment for the "Silent Killer"*

21. *The Wonders of Water: How H2O Can Transform Your Life*

22. *INFUSION: 30 Delicious and Easy Fruit Infused Water Recipes for Weight Loss, Detox, and Vitality*

23. *The Ultimate Juice Cleanse: 25 Select Juicing Recipes to Optimize Weight Loss, Detox and Longevity*

24. *ADHD Explained: Natural, Effective, Drug-Free Treatment For Your Child*

25. *Confidence Explained: A Quick Guide to the Powerful Effects of the Confident and Open Mind*

26. *How to Help an Alcoholic: Coping with Alcoholism and Substance Abuse*

27. *Vitamin D Explained: The Incredible, Healing Powers of Sunlight*

28. *Last Call: Understanding and Treating the Alcoholic Brain (A Personal and Practical Guide)*

29. *Hooked: Life Lessons of an Alcoholic and Addict (How to Beat it Before it Beats YOU)*

30. *Fragmented: Piecing Together the Mind of an Addict*

31.Neuro-Linguistic Programming Explained: Your Definitive Guide to NLP Mastery

32.Hooking Up: A College Guy's Guide to Wild Fun, Casual Sex, and Campus Companionship

33.Natural Weight Loss: PROVEN Strategies for Healthy Weight Loss & Accelerated Metabolism

34. BEAT The Hangover: Your Ultimate Guide to Drinking, Partying and Waking up Hangover Free

Printed in Great Britain
by Amazon